GREEK GODS

Other Greek Gods

BY

Stephan Weaver

© 2017 Copyright

TABLE OF CONTENTS

Introduction

On Mount Olympus lived the twelve Olympian gods and goddesses who presided over the cosmos. These deities were responsible for maintaining order and following a regime that secured peace and longevity of life both on earth and Mount Olympus.

But the responsibility these deities burdened could not have been maintained were it not for the help of their minions and the other lesser gods such as Eros, Nike, Hades, the Muses, Nemesis, Morpheus and Adonis.

This eBook discusses twelve of the other Greek gods, relating stories that are not only beguiling but also redolent of the characters of each deity.

CHAPTER I

ADONIS

Adonis is the god of vegetation, life, birth and rebirth. He was also the prince of Cypriot. He is viewed as the archetype of a handsome man.

The deity, abounded with irresistible good looks, managed to ignite a war between the female goddesses Aphrodite and Persephone who—ironically, or rather strangely—were also his caretakers in his upbringing.

He is probably most celebrated because of the myth of his rebirth. In the middle of the summer, Athenian women would cultivate herbs that would spring fast from seed and perish shortly after. This ritual was known as the "Festival of Adonis." It was a festivity symbolic of the life of Adonis for whom they wailed and flailed.

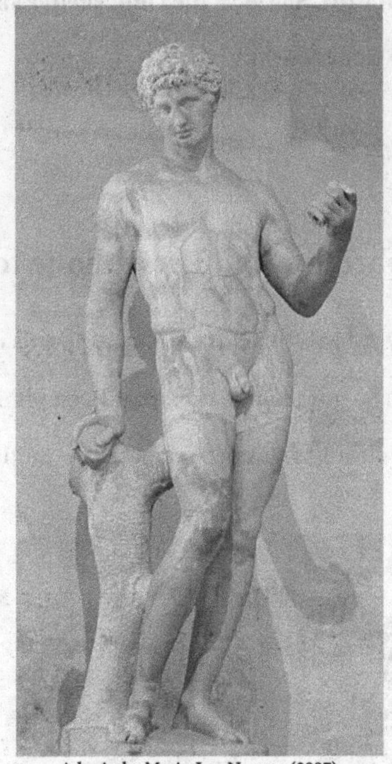

Adonis, by Marie-Lan Nguyen (2007)

The Birth of Adonis

The ruler of Syria, Theias, was seduced and tricked in to sleeping with his daughter, Princess

Smyrna (Myrrha). (Aphrodite is strongly linked to the spell cast on Smyrna which drove her to

this action.) Once the king found out about Smyrna's true identity he was enraged. He tried

killing her, but Smyrna pleaded for the help of the gods. They answered her prayers and

disguised her as a myrrh tree.

Smyrna, who was pregnant from the incident, gave birth to Adonis as the myrrh tree. Upon

discovering the new-born child, Aphrodite becomes spellbound by Adonis, perhaps because she was struck by the arrows of Eros. She gave the child shelter and then handed him to Persephone to be raised in the underworld.

The Brawl between Aphrodite and Persephone for Adonis' Love

The two guardians of the baby Adonis turn lovers. Once Adonis reached a certain age, he became irresistibly handsome. So gorgeous was he that Persephone refused to give him back to Aphrodite. This ignited a tumultuous fight between the two deities.

Venus and Adonis, by Titan (between 1555 and 1560)

The king of all gods, Zeus intervened to settle the dispute. He emerged with the solution to have the two goddesses share Adonis. The god of vegetation was to spend a third of the year in the underworld with Persephone and a third with Aphrodite. Zeus granted him the remaining one third of the year for himself but Adonis chose to spend it with Aphrodite. The two were deeply in love; they had a daughter named Beroe, after whom the city of Beirut (Berytos) was named.

Beroe would later be the love interest of the Olympian gods Poseidon and Dionysus and in the end become the consort of Poseidon.

The Death of Adonis

The death of Adonis is a contentious subject. He was killed by a boar which is believed to be sent by some deity. According to some accounts, it was Aphrodite's lover Ares who was jealous of their love that killed him. Others maintain that it was Apollo who wanted to avenge the goddess for blinding his son Erymanthus. Artemis, who always envied Adonis for his unmatched, hunting skills, is also proposed as the conspirator.

On the brink of his death, Adonis moaned squirming in pain. Aphrodite rushed to his rescue but he died in the crook of her arms. She peppers his blood with nectar and from this emerged the anemone. This is why the Adonis River (otherwise called Nahr Ibrahim or Abraham River), located in Lebanon, turns red every spring; it is the blood of Adonis that springs from the venerated Afqa.

The death of Adonis, by Luca Giordano (1684-1686)

CHAPTER II

THE GRAEAE

The Graeae, translated as "the grey sisters" or "the old women", were two or, according to some, three sisters. They were named Pemphredo ('alarm') and Enyo ('waster of cities'). Pseudo-Apollodorus adds a third one, Deino ('dread' or 'the warlike'). Hyginus' account even lists a fourth Graeae, Persis or Perso ('destroyer, slayer').

The siblings were children of the sea-gods Phorcys and Ceto. There is a farrago of depictions of them. In some accounts, the Graeae are described as grey crones; in others poetic works they are depicted as beautiful women. In the literary works of Aeschylus, the Graeae are describes as siren-shaped creatures with arms and heads of an aged women and a body shaped like a swan.

Hesiod depicts them as follows:

"And to Phorkys (Phorcys) Keto (Ceto) bore the Graiai (Graeae), with fair faces and gray from birth, and these the gods who are immortal and men who walk on the earth call Graiai, the gray sisters, Pemphredo robed in beauty and Enyo robed in saffron."

The Graeae were grey from birth, the sea's white foams embodied them. They only had one detachable tooth and eye which they had to share.

The Graeae were sisters and guardians of the Gorgons, the triad of sisters with snake hair. They watched the land of the Gorgons and kept them safe when they slept.

The Heist of Persues

Persues was inadvertently held to the promise of giving Polydectes a gift of his desire. Polydectes requested for the head of one of the Gorgons, Medusa. Persues was thus dogged to behead Medusa; the only thing that stood between him and his objective was the vigilant protectors of the monsters— the Graeae.

Persues was steeped in hate for the Phorcydes, it is most radiant in the writing of Aeschylus when he relates a point where Persues forewarns Io as she makes her treacherous journeys:

"Prometheus (Persues) warns Io of the perils she will face in her journey:] First, to you, Io, will I declare your much-vexed wandering, and may you engrave it on the recording tablets of your mind. When you have crossed the stream that bounds the two continents [probably the Red Sea], toward the flaming east, where the sun walks . . ((lacuna)) crossing the surging sea until you reach the Gorgonean plains of Kisthene (Cisthene), where the Phorkides (daughters of Phorkys) dwell, ancient maids (dênaiai korai), three in number, shaped like swans (kyknomorphoi), possessing one eye amongst them and a single tooth; neither does the sun with his beams look down upon them, nor ever the nightly moon. And near them are their three winged sisters, the snake-haired Gorgones (Gorgons), loathed of mankind, whom no one of mortal kind shall look upon and still draw breath. Such is the peril that I bid you to guard against."

Different accounts exist of how exactly Persues killed Madusa, but his fascinating heist of the Graeae is a tower of intrigue. He was instructed by Athena to find the Hesperides, the nymphs that shielded the orchard of Hera. They were the only ones with the weapons needed to bring the Gorgons to an overwhelming defeat. The Graeae knew where the Hesperides were, so he sat silently observing the Graeae pass their one eye around. He then crept up behind them and snatched the eye from one sister. The blind Graeae had no choice but to submit to his request.

According to some accounts, he ransomed the eye to coerce the sisters to tell him the whereabouts of the Hesperides and the Graeae did exactly that. Persues then returned their only eye back.

Perseus returning the eye to the Graeae

He got the weapon (the knapsack or Kibisis) from the Hesperides. Zeus, Athena and Hades provided him with a sword (Harpe), a helm of darkness and a polished shield. Fully accoutered, Persues carried out the task of beheading Medusa successfully.

Other accounts relate a different version of the event. According to them, Persues threw the eye of the Graea in Lake Tritonis thereby blinding the guards of the Gorgons, and slaying the sleeping Medusa.

Nonnus chronicles the event as follows:

"[Persues] had taken the travelling eye of Phorkys' (Phorcys') old one-eyed daughter unsleeping [the Graia, Graea]; he dived into the dangerous cave [of the Gorgones], reaped the hissing harvest by the rockside, the firstfruits of curling hair, sliced the Gorgon's teeming throat and stained his sickle red."

Perseus by Benvenuto Cellini (2005)

CHAPTER III

EROS

Most commonly known to us as Cupid, Eros was the mischievous god of attraction and sexual desire. According to the early works of Hesiod, Eros was a cosmic, primordial god who was created for the sole purpose of procreation. Then in his later works, Hesiod places Eros and another love god, Himeros, at the scene of Aphrodite's birth from the sea foam. According to this account it is suggested that Aphrodite was pregnant with Eros from the gentiles of Ouranos when she was born.

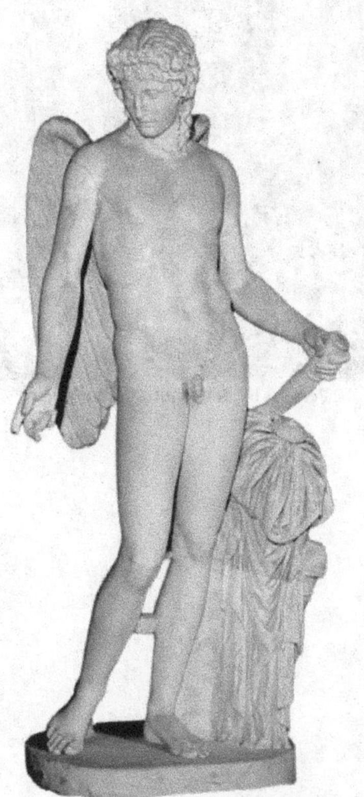

Eros Farnese, by Haiduc (date unknown)

Nonnus, on the other hand, proposes that Ares and Aphrodite were the parents of Eros.

What is indisputable though, is the umbilical attachment Aphrodite and Eros had. He accompanied her constantly and often served as her minion.

Equipped with his bow and arrows, Eros would ignite an irrepressible torrid of love within both mortals and gods. He was the pristine god of sensual love. His arrows, kept in his golden quiver, would have various powers: the golden ones would kindle love in the subjects they struck and the blunt, lead ones would stir up hate in a lover.

But Eros did more than kindle love and hate; he also tamed tigers and lions, robed Heracles' arms, broke Zeus' thunderbolts, and enjoyed his constant tug of wars with the aquatic creatures.

In works of art, Eros is often depicted as a child (a winged putto) with his bow and arrows, flower, sash and hare. Other symbols of Eros are kisses, wings, candles and cupids.

Initially, there was only one Eros or Cupid, but poets and artists of antiquity multiplied him into a legion of Erotes and Cupids.

The Birth of Eros

As discussed earlier, Hesiod, in his earlier works, depicted Eros as a primordial god who came into existence after Gaia (mother earth), Tartarus (the Underworld or Abyss) and Chaos.

Other literary sources of antiquity maintain that Eros was the son of Night (Nyx).

Aristophanes chronicles the birth of Eros as follows:

"At the beginning there was only Chaos, Night (Nyx), Darkness (Erebus), and the Abyss (Tartarus). Earth, the Air and Heaven had no existence. Firstly, black-winged Night laid a germless egg in the bosom of the infinite deeps of Darkness, and from this, after the revolution of long ages, sprang the graceful Love (Eros) with his glittering golden wings, swift as the whirlwinds of the tempest. He mated in the deep Abyss with dark Chaos, winged like himself, and thus hatched forth our race, which was the first to see the light."

Eros and his Soulmate Psyche

Psyche was a stunning princess whose spellbinding beauty had men throng to her worship. This upset Aphrodite whose altar was left empty as a result. So she sends Eros, her devout acolyte, to strike Psyche with his arrows and have her fall in love with the most grotesque creature on earth. He sets out to carry the task but instead becomes mesmerized by the mortal princess.

Cupid and Psyche, by François Gérard (1798)

He takes her away to his home and the two lovebirds start a beautiful life together. But one visit from Psyche's malicious sister changes everything. She convinces Psyche to betray her husband. This breaks the heart of Eros and has him leave his wife. Psyche, on the other hand, travels from pillar to post in seek of her lost husband. When she runs out of recourses, she pleads for the help of Aphrodite.

Aphrodite subjects her to a legion of grueling tasks, all of which Psyche completes successfully— off course, this was thanks to the supernatural help she received. At this point

Aphrodite gives in and allows her to return to her beloved Eros. Together they had a child named Voluptas or Hedone (physical pleasure).

Psyche, meaning 'butterfly' in Greek, was portrayed with butterfly wings. Psyche, having the English meaning "the human soul, spirit or mind", was a deification of the human soul.

CHAPTER IV

HADES

Son of Cronus and brother of Zeus, Hera, Poseidon, Hestia and Demeter, Hades was the god of the underworld, the dead and wealth. He was amongst the siblings who were swallowed by Cronus. The Titan God took this preemptive measure to thwart the usurpation by his children; this was prophesied by his mother Gaia.

Hades, Perhelion (2011)

During Zeus' feat of overthrowing the Titan Gods from their throne (this decade-long battle was known as the Titanomachy), Hades was the last sibling to be regurgitated by his father. After the success of the rebellion, the triad of brothers Poseidon, Zeus and Hades drew lots to share the universe: Hades drew a terrible lot and ended up becoming the ruler of the underworld and the dead.

Although Hades was the ruler of the underworld, he was not viewed as death himself; another god, known as Thanatos, was believed to be the microcosm of death. He was nonetheless, feared by the Greeks as he was a rapacious god who always sought to expand his subjects; in fact, he favored those that wreaked havoc on earth and caused deaths. The Greeks avoided uttering his name in fear of incurring death; so much so that they used various euphemisms to refer to him. Pluto meaning "wealth" or Ploutodótēs meaning "giver of wealth" were amongst his many names.

His title "Pluto" also emanated from the belief that from the underground or abode (soil) sprung riches such as metal, crops etc. Sophocles, on the other hand, had a different way of depicting Hades' wealth. Referring to his as 'the rich one', he says:

"The gloomy Hades enriches himself with our sighs and our tears."

In fear of his wrath and in hope of warding off the spirit of the dead, the people of Greece would appease Hades with an array of sacrifices, including black sheep, and other dark-furred animals. Those making the rituals would also drip their blood into a fissure or pit on the ground. During these sacrifices the person would always turn his/her face away.

Hades was often depicted with Cerberus, his three-headed dog, and a pitchfork with which he would conjure earthquakes.

Persephone's Abduction

The gorgeous daughter of Demeter, Persephone was abducted and taken to the underworld by Hades when she was gathering flowers from the meadows of Nysa.

Hades Abduction, by an unknown painter (18th Century)

Enraged by the acts of Hades, Demeter descended upon the earth the curse of a relentless famine. So harsh was the famine that each deity implored she lift the curse before it pulverized the human race. She vowed to see this to the end until she saw her daughter again.

The gravity of the situation caught Zeus' attention and he intervened through Hermes who asked Hades to return Persephone.

Persephone returned to her mother, but not completely. Before she departed from the underworld, Hades fed her sweet pomegranate seed that was to bind her to him for eternity.

Upon her return Demeter asked her daughter:

"...but if you have tasted food, you must go back again beneath the secret places of the earth, there to dwell a third part of the seasons every year: yet for the two parts you shall be with me and the other deathless gods."

And it was thus arranged that Persephone spend a third of the seasons in the underworld with Hades. The mourning of the grieving mother brought "winter" to earth.

Persephone, however unwillingly, became the consort of Hades.

Hades Entraps Theseus and Pirithous

Theseus and Pirithous had a rather lofty plan: to abduct and marry Helen and Persephone, Zeus' two daughters. Theseus desired Helen. They both managed the successful bid of kidnapping her and hiding her away at Aethre's place (the mother of Theseus), until she reached an able age for marriage.

The duo journeyed to the underworld for their next objective: Persephone. Privy of their treacherous plan to capture his wife, Hades welcomed them to his realm warmly.

He offered them a lovely banquet and they rushed to feast. As the two sat on the chairs they were instantly ensnared by a clutch coiling snakes that bound them to the seats.

Heracles helped Theseus escape from Hades but Pirithous remained a captive for his audacity in desiring a god's wife.

CHAPTER V

NIKE

In Greek Mythology, Nike is defined as the goddess of victory, speed and strength. Daughter of Styx (Ocean's daughter) and Pallas (a Titan), Nike is often depicted with wings— hence why she was also called the "Winged Goddess". There are also representations of her in the ancient arts together with other gods.

A stone carving of the Goddess Nike, by Maxfield

Nike was the sister of Bia (Force), Zelus (Zeal) and Kratos (Strength).

The goddess was the subject of the most celebrated figures of ancient Greek arts. Nike (also called Victoria by the Romans) appeared on pottery, sculpture and coins. The sculpture of Nike with wings in Delos is the oldest surviving relic, which is dated to 550 BC. Archermos is reported to have been the one who sculpted it. The essence of the archaic period exists in the statue with the common pose of running and bent knees.

The goddess Nike always had close associations with the goddess Athena. Athena's statue in Parthenon depicts Athena holding Nike in her hand.

There are also appearances of the goddess Nike on other ornamental sculptures. There were also establishments of statues dedicated to the goddess for the commemoration of military victories.

The goddess didn't possess much of a distinctive myth of her own like the many deities.

Nike Participates in the Battle of the Titans

The king of Mount Olympus, Zeus, was amassing forces against the older deities for the Titan War. Styx, Nike's mother, brought her four offspring, Zelus, Nike, Bia and Kratos to the god Zeus to assist him in the war.

Nike was chosen for the position of a charioteer in the battle of the Titans, whilst her other siblings were appointed Zeus' sentinels.

The victors were rewarded fame and glory in the battlefield by the winged goddess Nike who flew around.

Zeus promised to make them live with him at Olympus forever. Hesiod puts it like this:

"And Styx the daughter of Okeanos (Oceanus) was joined to Pallas and bare Zelos (Emulation) and trim-ankled Nike (Victory) in the house. Also she brought forth Kratos (Cratus, Strength) and Bia (Force), wonderful children. These have no house apart from Zeus, nor any dwelling nor path except that wherein God leads them, but they dwell always with Zeus the loud-thunderer. For so did Styx the deathless daughter of Okeanos plan on that day when the Olympian Lightener called all the deathless gods to great Olympus, and said that whosoever of the gods would fight with him against the Titans, he would not cast him out from his rights, but each should have the office which he had before amongst the deathless gods. And he declared that he who was without office and rights as is just. So deathless Styx came first to Olympus with her children through the wit of her dear father. And Zeus honored her, and gave her very great gifts, for her he appointed to be the great oath of the gods, and her children to live with him always. And as he promised, so he performed fully unto them all."

CHAPTER VI

NEMESIS

Nemesis was the goddess who was perceived by many as ruthless. This was because she was the goddess of revenge for deeds considered vice and good fortunes that weren't due.

Nemesis, by Alfred Rethel (1837)

Her wrath was most shown to humans who committed hubris (an act of arrogance towards the deities). Happiness and unhappiness were measured by her and those with inordinate wealth and fortune suffered with losses, as she thought no one deserved inordinate good. This was done to make humans humble. Such acts of Nemesis towards human affairs were to maintain balance.

Other names she was often called by were "Goddess of Rhamnous" and "Adrasteia." Nemesis' name initially meant the distributor of both reward and punishment.

According to Hesiod, Erebus and Nyx (Night) were the parents of Nemesis, though, in other accounts, she was depicted as Zeus or Oceanus' daughter.

In Greek's work of art, Nemesis was depicted as a goddess with wings who put on a crown in her hair. A dagger or a whip was also a part of her representation in Greek arts. Though she was a minor deity in the Pantheon of Greek, the empires of Rome and Greek considered her a cult figure. She was summoned by both humans and gods to pay revenge on the culpable, the vain and the ones with too much fortune.

Nemesis Punishes Narcissus

One famous myth of Nemesis includes the punishment of Narcissus.

Narcissus was a young man blessed with beauty— a beauty which kindled love in the hearts of many. But Narcissus was an arrogant hunter who gave no respect or love to those who had affection for him. Nemesis was summoned by one of his rejected admirers to punish him with the ache of unreciprocated love. Nemesis gladly did so.

Narcissus was led to a pool by Nemesis; there, upon seeing his reflection from the water, he fell in love with himself just like his other admirers. He didn't realize it was just an image. Owing to the love Narcissus had for his own reflection, he was unable to move away from it and died out of starvation there eventually. His body was turned into a flower as punishment for his selfishness and vanity.

Nemesis lays an Egg, where Helen of Troy was born

Helen of Troy, in many myths, is described as the child of Leda and Zeus. But it was widely accepted that the mother of Helen was Nemesis.

Nemesis was one of the women the king of the gods, Zeus, pursued. Nemesis made various endeavors to avoid him by turning in to different creatures but ended up failing.

To escape Zeus, she took a form of a goose one time, but he mated with her as he in turn took a form of a swan. The goddess, while still a goose, laid an egg. The egg was founded by a herdsman in the foliage's; he gave it to Leda. The egg was placed in a box by Leda up to the moment Helen hatched. Leda raised her as her own— hence why she was called Helen's mother.

Nemesis Robs Aura of her Virginity

Aura, Artemis' close companion, boastfully teased the goddess Artemis that her virginity was superior to that of the goddess. The humiliated Artemis went to Nemesis for consultation. The goddess of vengeance declared that the fitted punishment for Aura was to deprive her of her maidenhood.

The god of love, Eros, was asked by Nemesis to make the god of sea, Poseidon, infected with lust. Eros struck Poseidon with his celebrated arrow and ignited an irrepressible lust for Aura.

Along the path of Aura, the bewitched Poseidon created a water spring which was enchanted. Aura drank the water and instantly fell asleep. The god of sea took this opportunity to rape her. Upon waking up, Aura was so enraged that she murdered numerous of villagers and even devoured one of her twin children.

CHAPTER VII

PAN

In Greek mythology, the half-human god, Pan, dwelled in Greek's forests and mountains.

Possessing a goat's horns, tail and legs, Pan was the god of hunting, the wild and the mountain.

He was also the god of flocks and shepherds, and rustic music.

Sweet, piercing, sweet was the music of Pan's pipe by Mary Macgregor (191?)

Who the exact parents of Pan were is still vague. Some myths claim Dionysus, Apollo, Zeus or Hermes might have been his father; while his mother might have been a nymph named Dryope. It is also assumed that Aphrodite or Penelope may have been his mother.

The god had special affections for nymphs and his attempt to seduce them often failed due to his unattractive look. Among the nymphs he adored were Syrinx, Pitys, Echo and Selene, the moon goddess. Other myths also indicate that Aphrodite was one of the women Pan had a romantic affection for.

The half-human god was associated with the word "panic". Pan had a very intimidating voice when he got angry, thus any hapless being that was close enough to get a taste of it was engulfed with panic.

Pan never had temples attributed to him. He, nevertheless, was worshiped in settings that were natural, caves being one. Caves dedicated for worship to the god included the cave in Mt. Parnassos, the Korkykeion cave, and the other in Attica, the Vari cave. There were sacrifices made to the god, particularly by shepherds, which often included kids, sheep or goats. There were also votive offerings made to the god such as a clay statue of petite herdsmen, lamps, vases and grasshoppers which were crafted out of gold.

Around 500BC, Pan began to appear in the art of Greek. On Greek Pottery, the god is often illustrated as a full goat in an upright stance on his back legs. He later on is represented as having an upper body and a human face but with horns of a goat in red-figure pottery.

Pan Invents the Musical Instrument Syrinx

According to Greek Mythology, Syrinx, a stunning nymph, crosses the path of Pan one day. She was the daughter of the river god, Ladon. The besotted god endeavored to seduce Syrinx, but she got successful escaping him. Syrinx went to Zeus to implore him to save her from being captured by him, and just when he did she was transformed into reeds by Zeus.

The reeds were smashed into pieces by the enraged god. But he was shortly devoured with remorse and kissed the fractured reeds as he wept. He discovered, while he was kissing the reeds, that his breath produced sounds from them. This is how he created the musical instrument which he named after his beloved nymph.

Pan Challenges Apollo and Looses

Pan once made the mistake of comparing Apollo's music to that of his and challenged the god of music to a contest. The mountain-god, Tmolus, was selected to judge. Pan began playing his Syrinx to which he and his devout follower, Midas, basked in the rustic melody. Apollo played next and was declared the winner by Tmolus. All were pleased with the judgment except Midas who believed that the award was unjust. Apollo, intolerable of Midas' discontented ears, turned them into a donkey's ear. The Roman poet, Ovid, describes the event like this:

"The sacred Mountain's (Mons) judgment and award pleased all who heard; yet one voice challenging, crass-witted Midas' voice, called in unjust. Delius [Apollon] could not suffer ears so dull to keep their human shape. He filled them with coarse grey hairs, and hinged their base to move and twitch and flop; all else was man; in that one part his punishment; he wears henceforth

a little ambling ass's ears. Disfigured and ashamed he sought to hide his temples with a clinging purple turban."

According to another account of the myth, there was a tie in the first round, therefore a second match was held. Apollo, in the second match, insisted they play their musical instruments upturned. Apollo was not affected at all while playing his lyre upside-down; whilst, on the other hand, Pan was finding difficulty producing sounds in that formation. Apollo, thus, ended up winning.

CHAPTER VIII

MORPHEUS

Morpheus, in Greek Mythology, was the god of dreams. His father was the god of sleep, Somnus. Morpheus had siblings which amounted to a thousand— known as the Oneiroi. His siblings included Phantasos and Phobetor.

Phobetor was considered to bring about nightmares, and had the ability of transforming into any gigantic and intimidating animal; and Phantasos was the creator of false and surreal dreams.

Contrary to these two siblings, the god Morpheus transfers prophesies and messages to the mortals from the gods.

Morpheus and Iris, by Pierre-Narcisse Guérin (1811)

Morpheus, the Dream Messenger

This god possessed the ability to take a human formation of any kind and make appearances in dreams (though his real form was a daemon with wings). Ovid states that Morpheus' talent was not just circumscribed to physically mimicking humans, but also extended to gait, mood, voices and speech. He was most favored by the gods for this reason.

In Metamorphosis, the great poet Ovid says:

"King Sleep was father of a thousand sons – indeed a tribe – and of them all, the one he chose was Morpheus, who had such skill in miming any human form at will. No other Dream (Oneiro, Morpheus' brother) can match his artistry in counterfeiting men: their voice, their gait, their face – their moods; and, too, he imitates their dress precisely and the words they use most frequently. But he mimes only men..."

The actual form of the god of dreams had wings on his back. Morpheus and his brothers are said to have gotten the wings from Thanatos, the god of death— also their uncle. According to some accounts, nevertheless, they were said to have been born with it.

Morpheus' use of his wings were not only limited to reaching those in seek of help in their dreams. He also used it to transport Somnus, his wingless father, to the caves in the Dream World. Morpheus' father was said to be a deity who was indolent— expending the majority of his day sleeping.

The Dream World

Morpheus' family dwelled in the Dream World. As the god of dream sent out messages to mortals and frequented numerous bedrooms, he used to sleep in a cave encircled by chock-full of poppy seeds.

The Dream World was the place where the River of Oblivion and River of Forgetfulness were found. Two monsters highly safeguarded the gates and effortlessly caused great terror to any visitor who was uninvited.

In Greek mythology, Morpheus did not have a wife, as he was by far the busiest god. According to other accounts, however, Morpheus had a relationship with Iris, the messenger of the gods and goddess of the rainbow.

CHAPTER IX

HECATE

Hecate, who is also known as Hekate or Trivia, was the mysterious yet mighty goddess of sorcery, the moon, the night, crossroads, necromancy, and much more. She is also known as a patron goddess of the Wiccans. Her connection with the dead and ghosts was also duly noted in various sagas.

Hecate, by William Blake (1795)

According to Hesiod, who was the first to declare her presence in literature, Hecate was the daughter, the only offspring of the mighty Titans, Asteria and Perses.

"Hecate whom Zeus the son of Cronos honored above all. He gave her splendid gifts, to have a share of the earth and the unfruitful sea. She received honor also in starry heaven, and is honored exceedingly by the deathless gods. For to this day, whenever anyone of men on earth offers rich sacrifices and prays for favor according to custom, he calls upon Hecate. Great honor comes full easily to him whose prayers the goddess receives favorably, and she bestows wealth upon him; for the power surely is with her. For as many as were born of Earth and Ocean amongst all these she has her due portion. The son of Cronos did her no wrong nor took anything away of all that was her portion among the former Titan gods: but she holds, as the division was at the first from the beginning, privilege both in earth, and in heaven, and in sea."

The goddess of sorcery is often illustrated as a woman with two burning torches in her hands. On some Greek vase painting she is illustrated as a woman wearing hunting boots and a skirt, an image that has much semblance to that of Artemis. She is also referred to as the "Mistress of Animals" and when referenced as such she is illustrated as a goddess with three animal heads – a dog, a horse and a lion.

Abduction of Persephone

Hecate has had quite a significant presence in various events. And one that she is famed for happens to be the moments that followed the abduction of Persephone, for which she was called the tender-hearted Goddess.

According to Homeric Hymn when Persephone was abducted by the daunting god of the Underworld, Hades, she used whatever energy she had to release a desperate cry for help. But no one, not even the mightiest god Zeus was able to hear her wail. Helios and Hecate, however, heard the scream but were unable to rescue her from her abductor.

Demeter then following her daughter's disappearance steeped in grief and began to roam the earth far and wide. For nine days consecutively she pursued this harsh journey of hers. But then on the 10th day, she was approached by the tender-hearted goddess, Hecate.

"Queenly Demeter, bringer of seasons and giver of good gifts, what god of heaven or what mortal man has rapt away Persephone and pierced with sorrow your dear heart? For I heard her voice, yet saw not with my eyes who it was. But I tell you truly and shortly all I know" Hecate said, holding two burning torches.

In seek of counsel, Demeter then, accompanied by Hecate, and went to Helios, who told them where Persephone was taken. The gods then decided to release Persephone from the underworld but only under the condition that she returns back to it annually. At this juncture Hecate decided to become her thoughtful companion, one who was willing to escort her to and from Hades' realm on a yearly basis.

As a result of this gracious deed, Hecate became known as the Eleusinian Mysteries Goddess.

CHAPTER X

THE MUSES

The Muses were one of the most fascinating beings in Greek Mythology. They were nine sisters, young, skillful and enchantingly beautiful. There are different accounts as to whose daughters they were; but what is commonly known is that they are the offspring of Mnemosyne and Zeus.

According to Hesiod Theogony, the Muses were brought to life at the base of Mount Olympus in Pieria.

Their name says all there is to say about the kind of deities they were—they simply inspire. The Muses were goddesses of poetry, dance, music, song, literature, science and much more. They were also deities of wisdom, ones who never forget the countless occurrences of bygone days.

Apollo and the Muses on Mount Helion (Parnassus), by Claude Lorrain (1680)

Distinctions of the Nine Sisters

The nine sisters, Calliope, Clio, Euterpe, Erato, Melpomene, Polyhymnia, Terpsichore, Thalia, and Urania had their own domains to govern.

Euterpe was the Muse that kindled melancholic poetry, music and song. She is often seen holding the "Aulos", which is an archaic musical instrument that has much semblance to that of a flute.

Clio was the goddess of "History". She is often depicted as one with books and scrolls in her hands. Clio, much like the nature of history, never forgot any of the things that had happened.

Thalia was the goddess of laughter – comedy was her domain of rule. She is illustrated as the Muse wearing a "Comic Mask".

The Muses: Clio, Euterpe and Thalia, by Eustache le Sueur (between 1652 and 1655)

Calliope was the Muse that inspired and cultivated "Epic poetry". In various paintings she is illustrated as a beautiful woman holding a "writing tablet".

Melpomene was the deity of heartbreak and tragedy. Ancient paintings often show her wearing a "Tragic Mask".

Erato was the Muse of Lyrical poetry. She is illustrated as woman wearing a tiara embellished by roses and holding an ancient musical apparatus called "Cithara", it has much semblance to that of a lyre.

Polyhymnia was the sister that inspired the creation of sanctified verses – hymns. She is known to be a goddess that always wore a veil and in a meditative mindset.

Urania was the scientific Muse of astronomy. Paintings show her holding the galactic globe and a compass.

Terpsichore was the Muse of harmonic dancing and song. Paintings of ancient Greece show her with a lyre in her hands and always dancing in profound harmony.

The Muses Melpomene, Erato and Polyhymnia, by Eustache le Sueur (between 1652 and 1655)

CHAPTER XI

JANUS

"I'm your best friend, I'm your worst enemy, I'm Janus, God of Doorways. Beginnings.

Endings. Choices."

Different depictions of Janus, Bernard de Montifaucon (2013)

Janus was a god like no other. He was the god of beginnings, passages, gates doors, transitions

and endings.

Janus is commonly characterized as having two faces that look at two opposite direction. According to scholars this is a depiction meant to illustrate the deities divine ability of looking to the past and future.

There are various accounts as to how Janus came to be known as a god. One says that he was the son of Ouranos and Terra. And the other claims that he was initially a mortal man. According to the latter account, Janus, when banished from Thessaly resided to Latium, where he met and got married to Camese. The newlyweds then had several children and he became the first ruler of Latium.

He built a new city on the coast of river Tiber and ruled the people in his kingdom for many years, leading them to a prosperity and civilization hitherto unknown. And when he died, he was turned into a god and Rome's staunch patron.

It is believed that the month January was named in honor of Janus.

Abduction of the Sabine Women

Janus' presence in Greek mythology is most radiant at the time when Romulus and his soldiers abducted the Sabine women. Following this abduction, the Sabine king, Titus, wanted retaliation and launched an assault on Rome.

Steeped in rage, Janus then instigated a volcanic eruption. And this outburst ended up killing Titus and several of his soldiers. For this partaking, the Romans honored Janus for years by leaving the doors of the walled but roofless edifice named "The Janus" were left wide open at times of war. This was a gesture meant to solicit assistance from Janus for the soldiers marching to war. And when the war would come to a conclusion and peace would prevail, the Romans would close these doors as a way of celebration.

CHAPTER XII

IRIS

Iris, who is also known as Arcus, was the Goddess of rainbow, of the sky and of the sea. But Iris was not just a goddess; she was also a harbinger of the gods and goddesses, especially for Hera and Hermes. She was known for transporting messages from one god to the other or from the gods to mortals.

Iris, by Luca Giordano (1684-1686)

An incident that shows her playing the part of a messenger was when in Homeric Hymn Zeus summoned her and requested she seek for Demeter to ask her to return to Mount Olympus.

"Demeter, father Zeus, whose wisdom is everlasting, calls you to come join the tribes of the eternal gods: come therefore, and let not the message I bring from Zeus pass unobeyed," Iris said.

She is often illustrated as a youthful and attractive maiden with divine golden-wings and holding a large jug with water in it – the water is said to have come from the "River Styx". In various ancient paintings Iris is also seen standing next to Olympian gods, usually Hera and Zeus, serving them either wine or honey.

Iris stands behind the seated Juno (right), by Wolfgang Rieger (2009)

Iris was the daughter of the marine god, Thaumas, and the cloud nymph, Elektra. She had four sisters, Aello, Ocypete, Celaeno and Arke. Iris later became the consort of the deity of the "West Wind", Zephyrus. And together they bore a son named Pothos.

Iris in the Titanomachy

During the epic battle of the Titans and the Olympians, which is commonly called "The Titanomachy", Iris' twin sister Arke decided to betray the Olympian Gods and become a harbinger of the Titans. Iris, on the other hand, stayed loyal to the Olympians.

This event created a wedge between the sisters and they, for the first time, became arch nemesis.

The twins had wings, Iris' was golden and Arke's was iridescent. But during the Titan War, Zeus punished Arke by ripping her gleaming wings away. The all mighty god Zeus then, as a wedding gift, gave those wings to Thetis. And Thetis later gave these magical entities to Achilles, her son, who is known to wear them on his feet.